P9-AOC-122

WITHDRAWN

Emma
Exclamation Point

Written by Barbara Cooper
Illustrated by Maggie Raynor

GARETH**STEVENS**
GS
PUBLISHING
A World Almanac Education Group Company

HUNTINGTON CITY-TOWNSHIP
PUBLIC LIBRARY
200 W. Market Street
Huntington IN 46750

Please visit our web site at: www.garethstevens.com
For a free color catalog describing Gareth Stevens Publishing's
list of high-quality books and multimedia programs, call
1-800-542-2595 (USA) or 1-800-387-3178 (Canada).
Gareth Stevens Publishing's fax: (414) 332-3567.

Library of Congress Cataloging-in-Publication Data

Cooper, Barbara, 1929-
    [Ethel Exclamation Mark]
    Emma Exclamation Point / written by Barbara Cooper; illustrated by Maggie
Raynor. — North American ed.
        p. cm. — (Meet the Puncs: A remarkable punctuation family)
    Summary: Introduces the use of the exclamation point through the story of
Emma, a member of the Punc family who, even as a child, had a long nose, a
button mouth, and a habit of speaking in exclamations.
    ISBN 0-8368-4225-1 (lib. bdg.)
    [1. English language—Exclamations—Fiction. 2. English language—Punctuation—
Fiction. 3. Teachers—Fiction.] I. Raynor, Maggie, 1946- , ill. II. Title.
PZ7.C78467Em   2004
[E]—dc22
                                        2004045218

This edition first published in 2005 by
Gareth Stevens Publishing
A World Almanac Education Group Company
330 West Olive Street, Suite 100
Milwaukee, Wisconsin 53212 USA

This U.S. edition copyright © 2005 by Gareth Stevens, Inc. Original edition
copyright © 2003 by Compass Books Ltd., UK. First published in 2003 as
(The Puncs) an adventure in punctuation: Ethel Exclamation Mark by Compass
Books Ltd.

Designed and produced by Allegra Publishing Ltd., London
Gareth Stevens editor: Dorothy L. Gibbs
Gareth Stevens art direction: Tammy West

All rights reserved. No part of this book may be reproduced, stored in a
retrieval system, or transmitted in any form or by any means, electronic,
mechanical, photocopying, recording, or otherwise, without the prior
written permission of the copyright holder.

Printed in the United States of America

1 2 3 4 5 6 7 8 9 08 07 06 05 04

Emma Exclamation Point

is the thinnest of
the Puncs.

rarf!

She is also
very tall !

Even as a baby,
she had a

long nose

and a

button mouth,

and her legs were like sticks!

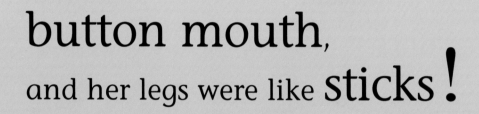

Goo!

When Emma's mother, Effie, saw her for the first time, she said, "Oh, dear!"

And her father, Eddie, said, "My goodness!"

Effie and Eddie live in a cottage near a river. They are always rushing down the path shouting

"No fishing!"
"No swimming!"

9

Eddie paints signs.

If you see one
of his signs,
you should read
the words very
carefully!

Emma's grandmother, Ethel, lives with Eddie and Effie. Ethel is very good with her hands. She sews fringes on curtains! When Emma was small, she used to love to watch her Grandma sew.

"Be careful, dear!"

Ethel used to say to Emma.

"Watch out for your fingers!"

While Ethel sewed, she would tell Emma stories about her great-great-great grandfather, Egbert, of the Philadelphia Puncs. Egbert was the friendliest Punc in Philadelphia!

"Hi, there!"

"Have a nice day!"

The Philadelphia Puncs

Emma is a teacher. She lives near the schoolhouse. A sign on her front gate says

"Beware of the dog!"

ruff!

Emma's dog's name is Elliott. He is a good watchdog! Elliott is not really fierce, but he has a very loud bark! His barking frightens away unwelcome visitors.

"Good boy, Elliott!"

Emma shouts to praise him.

Emma loves animals! Sometimes,
it seems that she is more kind-hearted
to animals than she is to humans!

People often hear Emma murmuring

"Poor little thing!"
"What a shame!"

"How sad!"

19

In the classroom, Emma knows exactly how to make her students behave themselves.

"Sit up straight!"

"Pay attention!"
"Open your books!"
"Stop talking!"

No one dares
disobey her!

Emma does not like to see her students reading comic books.

"Absolute nonsense!"

"Utter rubbish!"

she cries.

And she certainly does not want them using words such as

zap! and splat! and pow!

Three times a week, Emma's students have a PPE (Punc Physical Education) class. Emma leads the exercises !

"Bend your knees!"
"Shoulders back!"
"Reach! Stretch!"

She secretly wants everyone to be as thin as she is !

Because Emma is so thin, she never feels warm!

"Brrr! It is very cold today!"

she grumbles, even when the Sun is boiling hot!

HUNTINGTON CITY-TOWNSHIP
PUBLIC LIBRARY
200 W. Market Street
Huntington IN 46750

27

Emma may be thin, but she enjoys eating a lot of food.

"How delicious!"

"What a treat!"

she exclaims, lunching on bacon, bread, and button mushrooms!

Emma especially enjoys cherry soda pop. She drinks it every day!

29

So, now you know!

If you want to say something

in a surprised way,

a worried way,

an excited way,

a bossy way,

a miserable way,

or a cheerful way,

you cannot do it

without the help of

Emma
Exclamation Point!

Emma's Checklist

- **Punctuate a greeting with an exclamation point:**
  Hi, there! Have a nice day!

- **Use an exlamation point to show shock or surprise:**
  Oh, dear! My goodness!

- **. . . disappointment or dismay:**
  Poor little thing! What a shame!

- **. . . enjoyment or approval:**
  How delicious! What a treat!

- **Quarrelsome speech is full of exclamation points:**
  Absolute nonsense!
  Utter rubbish!

- **An exclamation point can tell you when someone is probably joking:**
  Sometimes, it seems that Emma is more kind-hearted to animals than she is to humans!

- **Teachers really like to use exclamation points, especially when they are correcting you:**
  Sit up straight! Pay attention!

- **. . . or when they are giving you instructions:**
  Bend your knees!
  Shoulders back!

- **Exclamation points are in lots of signs and notices:**
  Beware of the Dog!
  No spitting!

- **. . . as well as in warnings:**
  Be careful, Emma!
  Watch out for your fingers!

- **Newspaper headlines often end with exclamation points:**
  Dog Bites Man!
  Punctown Weather Boiling Hot!

- **Exclamation points are very popular in cartoons, comics, and advertisements, especially after sound effects:**
  Zap! Splat! Pow!